DISNEY · PIXAR

COCO

The Essential Guide

Written by Glenn Dakin

Based on an original screenplay by Adrian Molina

Contents

"I gotta seize my moment!" Miguel

8

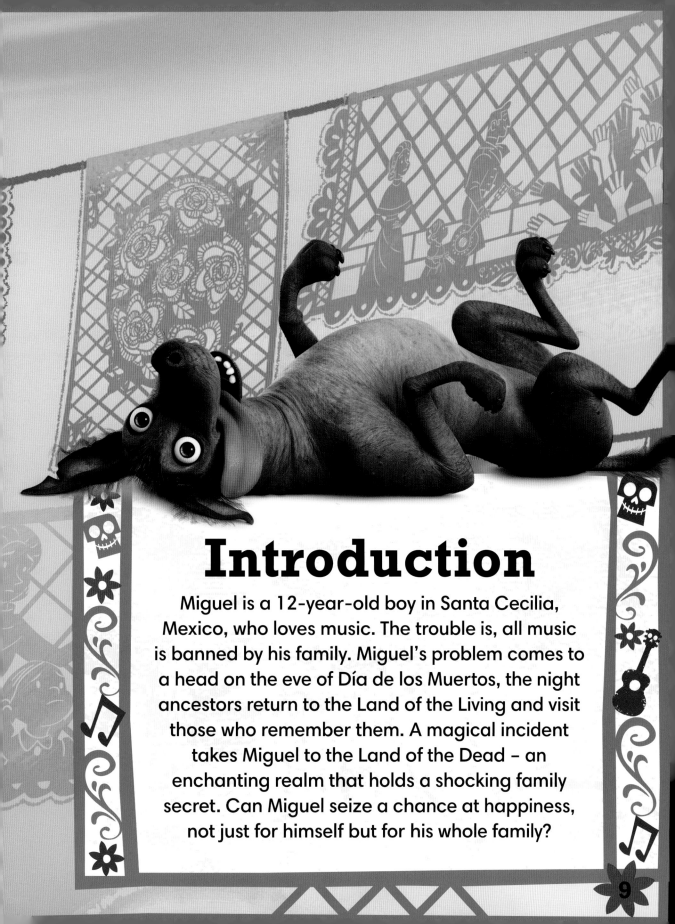

Introduction

Miguel is a 12-year-old boy in Santa Cecilia, Mexico, who loves music. The trouble is, all music is banned by his family. Miguel's problem comes to a head on the eve of Día de los Muertos, the night ancestors return to the Land of the Living and visit those who remember them. A magical incident takes Miguel to the Land of the Dead – an enchanting realm that holds a shocking family secret. Can Miguel seize a chance at happiness, not just for himself but for his whole family?

Miguel

This talented 12-year-old thinks he was born under a curse – his family hates music and banned it from the Rivera household. The problem is, music is Miguel's greatest passion. He doesn't want to fight with his family, but can he find a way to bring music into his home?

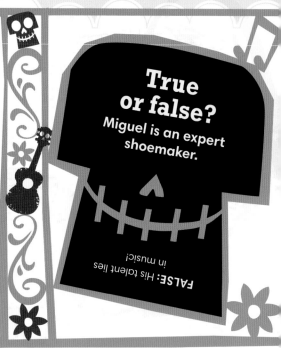

True or false?
Miguel is an expert shoemaker.

FALSE: His talent lies in music!

Talent contest
Miguel's heart leaps when he sees the poster for a Día de los Muertos talent show in the town plaza. Could this be his chance to follow his musical destiny?

Family secret
In an old family photo, Miguel finds his great-great-grandfather holding the guitar of musician Ernesto de la Cruz! Could they be the same man? Miguel shouts from the rooftops about his discovery.

Boots made by the Rivera family

Music mad

A magical mishap gives Miguel the opportunity to prove he can be a true musician – and to meet his idol Ernesto de la Cruz!

Skull decorations adorn guitar

"I'm supposed to play music!"

Guitar is his prized possession.

Surprising encounters

It isn't just Miguel who gets a shock when he wanders into the Land of the Dead. As a living boy, he's just as surprising to the spirits that he meets!

Hard-wearing denim jeans

Have you heard?

Coco can be forgetful. Sometimes she calls Miguel "Julio" by mistake! He doesn't mind a bit!

11

Día de los Muertos

Mexico's national holiday, Día de los Muertos (or Day of the Dead), is a time to celebrate the memories of your ancestors. Families come together to share stories about their loved ones. Graves are cleaned, while ofrendas (family shrines) are decorated with cherished photos.

Lights and love

At night during the celebration, families decorate the graves and tombs of their dead ancestors. Flowers, candles, incense and sweets turn the graveyard into an enchanted place.

Have you heard?

Colourful paper patterns displayed on the day are called "papel picado". These feature many different types of illustrations and designs.

"The petals guide our ancestors home."

Mamá

12

A path of petals

The bright orange marigolds of Mexico are known as the flowers of the dead. The aroma of the petals is said to lead the spirits home to be with their families again.

True or false?

Día de los Muertos is celebrated in the summer.

FALSE: It is celebrated in the autumn.

Bright orange marigolds adorn the ofrenda.

Family altar

Ofrendas are home-made altars created in honour of dead family members. They include a photo of the loved one and some of their favourite things to make them feel at home.

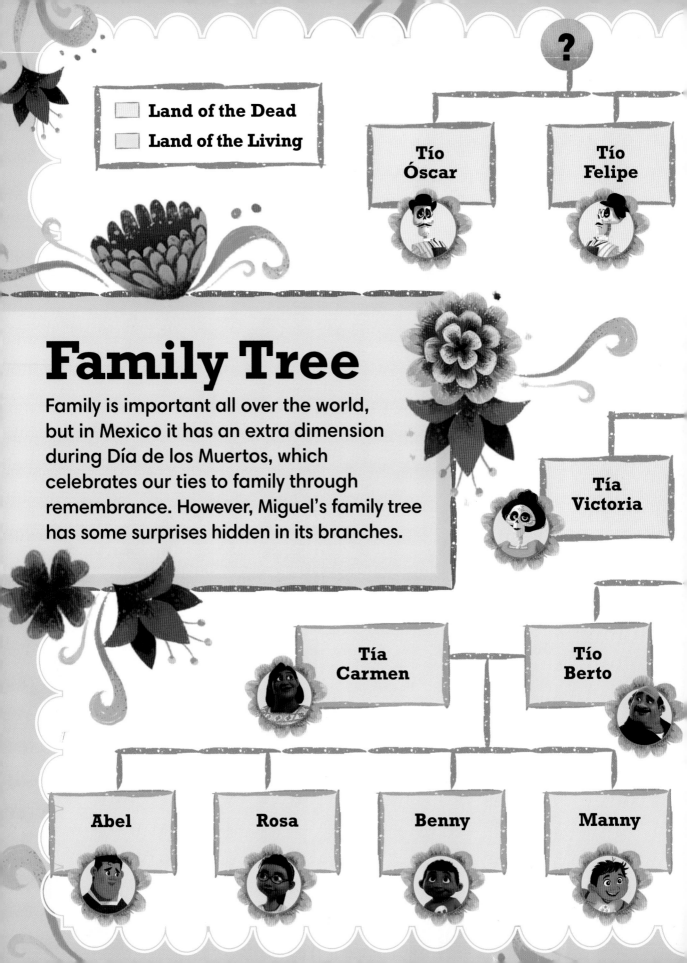

Family Tree

Family is important all over the world, but in Mexico it has an extra dimension during Día de los Muertos, which celebrates our ties to family through remembrance. However, Miguel's family tree has some surprises hidden in its branches.

Land of the Dead
Land of the Living

?

Tío Óscar

Tío Felipe

Tía Victoria

Tía Carmen

Tío Berto

Abel

Rosa

Benny

Manny

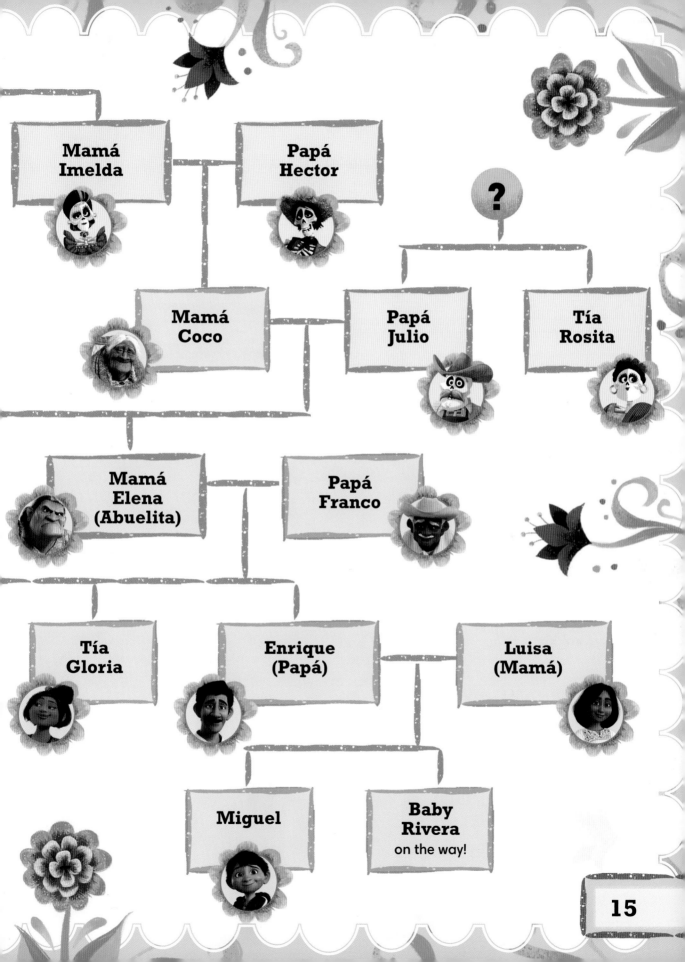

Mamá Imelda

Papá Hector

?

Mamá Coco

Papá Julio

Tía Rosita

Mamá Elena (Abuelita)

Papá Franco

Tía Gloria

Enrique (Papá)

Luisa (Mamá)

Miguel

Baby Rivera
on the way!

15

Abuelita and Mamá Coco

Miguel has plenty of doting female figures to make sure he is raised the right way. His grandmother, Abuelita, runs the house like a ship's captain. Her mother, Mamá Coco, is someone everyone can tell their troubles to.

Cut out

The face of Coco's father has been ripped out of this old photo. It's a reminder that he vanished from her life.

Long, plaited hair

Musical miracle

When Miguel finally does play for Coco, all the musical memories of her childhood come flooding back.

Link to the past

The oldest surviving Rivera, Mamá Coco is the only living link to the family's dramatic history. And she doesn't remember too well these days!

Dress with traditional Mexican embroidery

Músico banned

Abuelita gets mad when a músico speaks to Miguel. She wants to protect her little angel from musicians.

Abuelita's famous stare

Tough love

Abuelita is so anti-music she even shuts the window if there's a van passing by with its radio on. She is proud of her cooking and loves to feed Miguel her tasty tamales.

"I'm hard on you, because I care, Miguel."

Abuelita

Have you heard?

Abuelita enforces the family ban on music that has been going on for generations.

Apron worn for chores

Workshop

Miguel's family runs the Rivera Family Shoemakers – one of the oldest and most respected shops in the little town of Santa Cecilia. It's a real family affair, with young and old members of the family pitching in to make sure the townspeople are well-heeled.

"It's time you joined us in the workshop!" Papá

Welcome aboard

Miguel is welcomed into the family shoe business on the eve of Día de los Muertos. His Papá believes that the family that works together stays together.

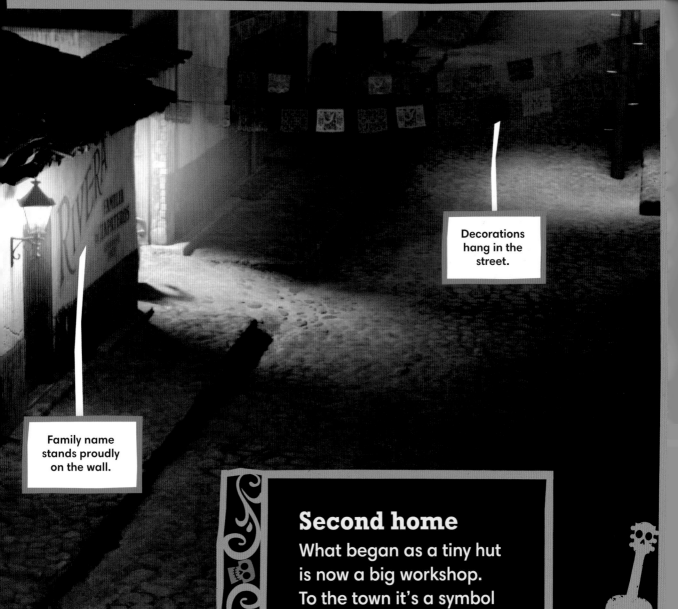

Decorations hang in the street.

Family name stands proudly on the wall.

Second home

What began as a tiny hut is now a big workshop. To the town it's a symbol of hard work, reliability and tradition.

19

The Rivera Family

Family comes first for the Riveras, and each member is cherished. Everyone knows their place in the pecking order, and while Papá is the boss in the workshop, he obeys Abuelita's rules at home. Nobody is taken for granted, or allowed to neglect their family duties!

Mighty Mamá
Abuelita is the head of the family. She keeps everyone in line and makes sure ancestors are remembered and honoured.

Mamá
(with another
Rivera on the way!)

Relatively shocking
Tía Gloria, Tío Berto and Tía Carmen are aghast when Miguel spills family secrets. Riveras hate gossip – about themselves or anyone else!

Papá
Franco

United generations
Riveras always stick together. From the very youngest to the more wrinkly members (like Papá Franco), everyone in this close group understands the importance of family.

"You have your family here to guide you... You are a Rivera." Papá

Abel

Miguel's cousins
Like their cousin Miguel, Abel and Rosa are still finding their path in the world. The older generation is never short of advice for the young.

Rosa

Benny

Papá

21

Hideout

When he needs to be alone with his dreams, Miguel retreats to his hideaway in a forgotten attic space. There he doesn't have to hide the secret in his heart – the fact that he loves music and is obsessed with Mexico's greatest musician, Ernesto de la Cruz.

De la Cruz record cover

Secret ofrenda

Hidden in the attic is Miguel's own private ofrenda, a display he created to remember his hero, de la Cruz. Vinyl records, sheet music, figurines, books and ticket stubs create a perfect tribute.

Guitar built from scrap

Candles for a hero

Miguel lights candles in memory of Ernesto. He, like all fans, welcomes the return of his hero's spirit. Little does he know what's in store for him this Día de los Muertos!

Best of de la Cruz
Most treasured of all is Miguel's video of the best moments from his hero's movies. Miguel doesn't just watch, he learns guitar chords and even Ernesto's poses as he performs.

"No more hiding!"
Miguel

De la Cruz figurine

Miguel owns every de la Cruz album.

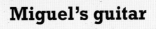

Miguel's guitar
The hideout is where Miguel plays his own guitar, a cobbled-together copy of Ernesto's famous instrument. It's made from a battered soundboard and other scavenged odds and ends.

Dante

This funny street dog loves to follow Miguel around. He's a hairless Mexican Xoloitzcuintli (sho-lo-eets-kweent-lee) – but you can call him a xolo (sho-lo) for short! Curious, friendly and unable to resist a new smell, Dante seems to pop up whenever Miguel is about to have an adventure.

Street survivor

This scrappy hound has learnt to survive on the street. He'll sniff any bag for food and even dance for a sweet bread roll!

Wispy hairs on ears and head

Enchanted Xolo?

He may look goofy but Dante has hidden depths. It is said that Xolo dogs have mysterious powers and guide the spirits.

True or false?
Dante was Miguel's birthday present.

FALSE: He's a stray.

> **"Never name a street dog. They'll follow you forever."**
> Abuelita

Tough, smooth skin

24

Dying for a snack

Ever-hungry Dante can't stop chasing food, even in the Land of the Dead. Well, the food there is classier than what he finds in the alleys back home!

Sharing secrets

Dante is the only friend Miguel can tell all his hopes and dreams to, and sing all his favourite songs with. Shh!

High spirits

Miguel once told Dante that he's no spirit guide. But after helping save Miguel's quest, Dante finally earns his wings.

Have you heard?

In his spirit-guide form, Dante resembles an "alebrije", which is a type of Mexican folk art.

Talent Show

Miguel is an unknown in the music world, but that could change overnight at the Día de los Muertos talent show. Music lovers come from far and wide to witness the stars of tomorrow. Miguel has one problem— Abuelita has smashed his guitar!

Eager Santa Cecilian audience

Mexican vihuela (five-stringed guitar)

Stars of tomorrow

As the time of the show gets nearer, a huge crowd gathers. Everyone hopes to see a new star born. Will they be watching the next Ernesto de la Cruz?

Not on the list

Performers have to provide their own instruments. Until Miguel can, the stage manager won't let him on the list of contestants.

Veracruz-style harp

Traditional Día de los Muertos calaca (skull) symbols

DÍA DE MUERTOS TALENT SHOW

PLAZA SANTA CECILIA · 7 PM

Guitar blues

Miguel is desperate to borrow a guitar so that he can play at the contest. But even the friendly músicos turn him away empty hande[d]

What Should Miguel Do?

Should Miguel follow his dream and try to be a great musician? Or should he listen to his family, forget music and join the shoemaking business? Only he can decide his own destiny.

REASONS TO FOLLOW TRADITION

❀ Everyone in my family is part of the business – it's what keeps us all together.

❀ They already gave me my own apron! That's kind of a special moment.

❀ Okay, let's face it, my Abuelita will be so angry if she finds out I play the guitar!

❀ It's a lot easier to do what everyone else wants.

❀ Papá will be so happy – he has always wanted me to work by his side.

> ## "You will listen to your family. No more music." Papá

REASONS TO FOLLOW MY DREAM

- 🍀 I LOVE music! It's everywhere. How can anyone ignore it?

- 🍀 I want to be just like my hero, the famous star Ernesto de la Cruz.

- 🍀 Suppose I'm just no good at making shoes?

- 🍀 Ernesto didn't hide his sweet skills – why should I have to hide mine?

- 🍀 Papá said the family spirits would guide me. Well, I'm pretty sure Ernesto IS family!

Ernesto de la Cruz

He started out as a nobody from the little town of Santa Cecilia and went on to become the most famous and loved musician in the land. He's now in the Land of the Dead where he leads a life that's as extravagant as it was when he was alive.

Immortal hero

Ernesto's statue stands in the plaza at Santa Cecilia where he took his first steps toward fame. Tour guides bring hundreds of fans there to worship his memory.

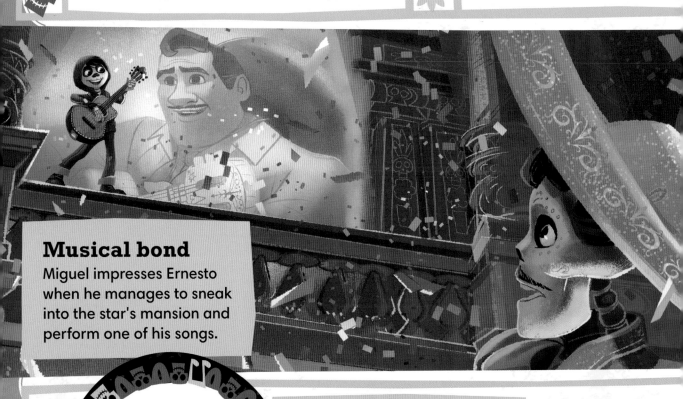

Musical bond

Miguel impresses Ernesto when he manages to sneak into the star's mansion and perform one of his songs.

Have you heard?

In his movies, de la Cruz did all of his own stunts. At least that's his story!

Fit for royalty

Rich beyond the dreams of his fans, Ernesto lived in a mansion that was more like a royal palace. The Land of the Dead contains an afterlife version.

Performs wearing a traditional sombrero.

Movie magic
De la Cruz is also remembered for the inspiring messages behind his many movies. He taught his fans that only a song has the power to change a heart.

"The rest of the world may follow the rules, but I must follow my heart!"

Man of the moment
Ernesto's message for the people of Mexico is to seize your moment. If the chance comes to change your life you should take it with both hands.

In the afterlife, de la Cruz wears an all-white suit.

True or false?
Ernesto placed his friends above all else.

FALSE: He showed no loyalty to his friends.

Ernesto's Tomb

There are many humble tombs in Santa Cecilia, but Ernesto de la Cruz's isn't one of them! Built on an extravagant scale, it looks fit for a king. His countless fans adorn the site with marigold petals, candles and other offerings to cherish his memory.

Tomb raider

Miguel is nervous about entering the tomb. But he believes he and Ernesto have a special connection, and that the musician would forgive him.

Have you heard?

The vibrant colour and strong smell of marigold flowers are believed to guide spirits home.

> **"Senõr de la Cruz? Please don't be mad ..."**
>
> Miguel

Legendary guitar

Miguel has a special reason for visiting Ernesto's tomb – it contains his famous skull-head guitar. And Miguel, on the night of the talent show, is a boy without a guitar.

Passing through

When Miguel is in Ernesto's tomb, he is startled by the arrival of a caretaker. He's even more shocked when the man passes right through him! Miguel has been turned into a spirit for taking from the dead.

Candles welcome the spirits.

Marigolds used to decorate the tomb.

Fans gather to remember the star.

Remember Me

The words of Ernesto's most famous song are inscribed on his tomb: "Remember Me". In Mexico, remembering the dead is what keeps their spirits with us.

33

Seeing Spirits

Miguel knows what Día de los Muertos is all about, but nothing could prepare him for the reality of seeing the spirit world. He's shocked to see ancestors visiting graves, inspecting shrines and even eating the treats left out for them.

Skeletons have detachable heads.

Shared fear

Miguel is terrified to find out he's surrounded by spirits. But that's okay, they are just as frightened of him. A living boy shouldn't be able to see them!

Grave incident

Miguel is so taken aback at joining the world of the dead that he tumbles into a grave. Now that he's a spirit, he should feel at home in there!

Graves decorated with flowers

In the spirit

Miguel soon learns that dead people are just as warm-hearted as the living. He can see the happiness the special day brings to family members – dead and alive.

Spirit glow around body

The Bridge

Miguel is amazed to see glowing bridges of marigold petals connecting the realm of the living and the Land of the Dead. These amazing structures allow the spirits of the dead to cross over and mingle with those on the other side who remember them.

"This isn't a dream then? You're all really out there." Miguel

Buildings piled on top of each other

Land of the Dead

As they cross the bridge, Miguel and Dante get their first glimpse of the wonders beyond. The shining city of the dead rises up before them.

Back to life

Miguel has no choice but to cross over. Only his relatives on the other side have the power to free him from his spirit form.

Old and modern buildings sit side-by-side.

Mystical mist shrouds the view.

True or false?

The dead can stay in the Land of the Living as long as they like.

FALSE: They must return by sunrise.

Dead Organised

Miguel discovers that on Día de los Muertos, thousands of spirits cross between the Land of the Living and the Land of the Dead. It's a massive operation, but rules, regulations and official departments make sure nothing goes wrong. Well, almost nothing ...

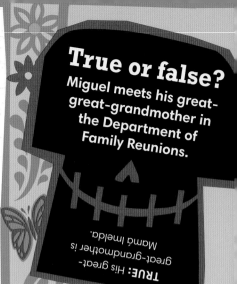

True or false?
Miguel meets his great-great-grandmother in the Department of Family Reunions.

TRUE: His great-great-grandmother is Mamá Imelda.

Arrivals and departures

Marigold bridges connect the Land of the Living to Grand Central Station, where all arrivals and departures are handled. This is where Mamá Imelda waits to find out why she can't cross over.

Grand Central

The Riveras stay close together through the busy hall of Grand Central Station. Luckily the dead handle holiday travel chaos with the right spirit.

Skull scanner

As he walks through the station's entry plaza, Miguel notices this monitor. It is used to scan those departing for the Land of the Living to check that they have been remembered. The scan must match a photo on an ofrenda somewhere.

Department of Family Reunions

If spirits, like Mamá Imelda, have travel problems of any kind they are sent to the Department of Family Reunions, where a clerk will look into their case. Family curses are a common cause of delays!

Welcome back

Those returning are greeted by the arrivals agent who asks if they have anything to declare. Usually they have food. Rarely do they have live boys!

Mamá Imelda

Mamá Imelda is the matriarch of the family and Miguel's great-great-grandmother. She began the family business when her musician husband abandoned her and their daughter, Coco. Miguel is astonished to meet her when he visits the Land of the Dead.

Vibrant paint decorates her skull.

Angry bones

Shoes have long been part of the Rivera family. Just like her granddaughter, Abuelita, Mamá Imelda uses them to express her emotions!

"You go home my way, or no way."

Leather cobbler's apron

Imelda's curse

It was this strong-minded woman who decreed that music would never be played again in the Rivera house. Alive or dead, she is not known for changing her mind.

True or false?

Mamá Imelda is a popular ancestor of the Rivera family.

TRUE: Although she was against music, she is much loved.

Family beauty

A treasured family photo captures Mamá Imelda when she was young and beautiful.

Photo bombshell

Mamá Imelda is furious when she discovers Miguel took her photo from the ofrenda. That's why she couldn't enter the Land of the Living!

Mixed blessing

It's so easy for Miguel to get home – he just needs Mamá Imelda's blessing before sunrise. She's happy to give it, as long as he gives up music forever!

Have you heard?

Mamá Imelda was once a great singer herself, and performed with her husband.

41

Hector

This scruffy skeleton is well known as a charming trickster in the Land of the Dead. But behind his scrappy surface lies a great sorrow. He is on the verge of being forgotten by his living daughter, and could soon disappear forever. Meeting Miguel could be his last hope.

Betrayed

When Hector quit touring with Ernesto, de la Cruz poisoned his drink. He left Hector dying and took the credit for his amigo's talent.

Talented team

Hector is a disguise artist – his disguise as the great Mexican artist, Frida Kahlo, was awesome! He shows Miguel a few tricks.

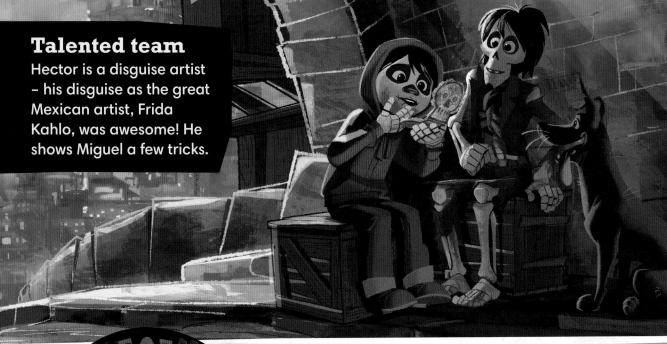

Have you heard?

Hector calls Miguel "chamaco", which is slang for boy or kid.

Showdown

Hector confronts de la Cruz, accusing him of stealing the songs that would have made the world remember him. Hector doesn't want revenge, only a chance to see his daughter.

Small, bandana-style neck scarf

Final curtain

Hector begins to fade away as Coco forgets him, and because he doesn't have a photo on an ofrenda. Miguel tells Mamá Imelda that her husband really did try to get home and hopes she can forgive him.

Braces hold up threadbare trousers.

True or false?
Hector's nickname is "Chorizo".

TRUE: Because friends think he died after choking on it.

Old bones becoming weaker

Funny bones

A natural entertainer, Hector knows how to get creative with his bones. He has plenty of tricks to make the most of his detachable limbs.

"I'm being forgotten!"

Rivera Ancestors

This close clan is still together in the Land of the Dead. Their favourite time of year is Día de los Muertos. They know their photographs will be put up on the family ofrenda and they can enjoy the festival in the Land of the Living. This year, however, proves more complicated!

Have you heard?
Mamá Imelda was banned from crossing the Marigold Bridge this year thanks to Miguel!

Tío Óscar

Travel chaos
The Riveras cause quite a stir when they turn up with a living boy at Grand Central Station. This is very unusual indeed!

True or false?
The Rivera ancestors are expecting to see Miguel.

FALSE: He should be in the Land of the Living!

Skeleton staff

The Rivera ancestors wear their cobbler's outfits in the Land of the Dead. This family is not afraid of hard work.

"I miss my nose."
Tío Óscar

Tía Victoria

Tío Felipe

Tía Rosita

Fiery Mamá
Mamá Imelda is a passionate matriarch. Being dead hasn't mellowed her one bit!

Papá Julio

Miguel's Mission

When Miguel finds himself in the Land of the Dead, he has to think quickly to get home by sunrise. He believes that in order to follow a musical destiny, he needs to get the blessing of Ernesto de la Cruz. He might just make it happen!

1

Helping Hector

Miguel makes a deal with Hector. If he can help Miguel meet de la Cruz, Miguel will put Hector's photo on the Rivera family ofrenda when he gets home.

3

Talent show

Hector tells Miguel that winning the talent show will give him a slot in Ernesto's Sunrise Spectacular. That's an all-access chance to meet de la Cruz.

4

Attention seeker

By singing one of Ernesto's songs at his mansion, Miguel believes he can grab the attention of the legendary star.

Master of disguise

Miguel uses Hector's paints to make himself blend in with the Land of the Dead. He can even walk like a skeleton!

Ernesto's blessing

Miguel manages to impress de la Cruz, before falling into his pool! This is where the plan begins to go a little off course.

De la Cruz's Mansion

High above the Land of the Dead stands the mansion of Ernesto de la Cruz – a symbol of wealth, fame and success. For Miguel, getting inside may be his only route home!

Miguel's moment

Inspired by de la Cruz's songs, Miguel summons the courage to perform for his hero. He sings that music is his language and the world is his family!

Party palace

The ultimate party destination if you've passed on, de la Cruz's mansion attracts all the A-listers of the afterlife. Inside there's a guitar shaped pool, and his movies are shown on a constant loop.

Lightshow can be seen for miles

Doorway to destiny
De la Cruz's home is like a golden beacon to Miguel, calling him to a fabulous destiny. A group of musicians smuggles the little músico in after hearing him play.

Lavish exterior hides serious security system.

Personal railway
De la Cruz's tower is so tall it has its own cliff railway to carry visitors up to the top. Skull-shaped doors echo the famous symbol on his guitar.

Service lift connects to all levels.

Towering success
It's not hard to find the mansion, it sits atop the tallest tower in the Land of the Dead. Only those with an invitation get past security.

Spirit Guides

One of the most spectacular sights in the Land of the Dead is the animal spirit guides that help souls find their way. These colourful creatures live double lives as plain or scruffy creatures in the living world.

Playing around
Although their job is serious, spirit guides are playful creatures. They leave phantom poop everywhere!

Giant wings enable passenger flight

Powerful tail

> **"They guide souls on their journey."**
>
> Tía Rosita

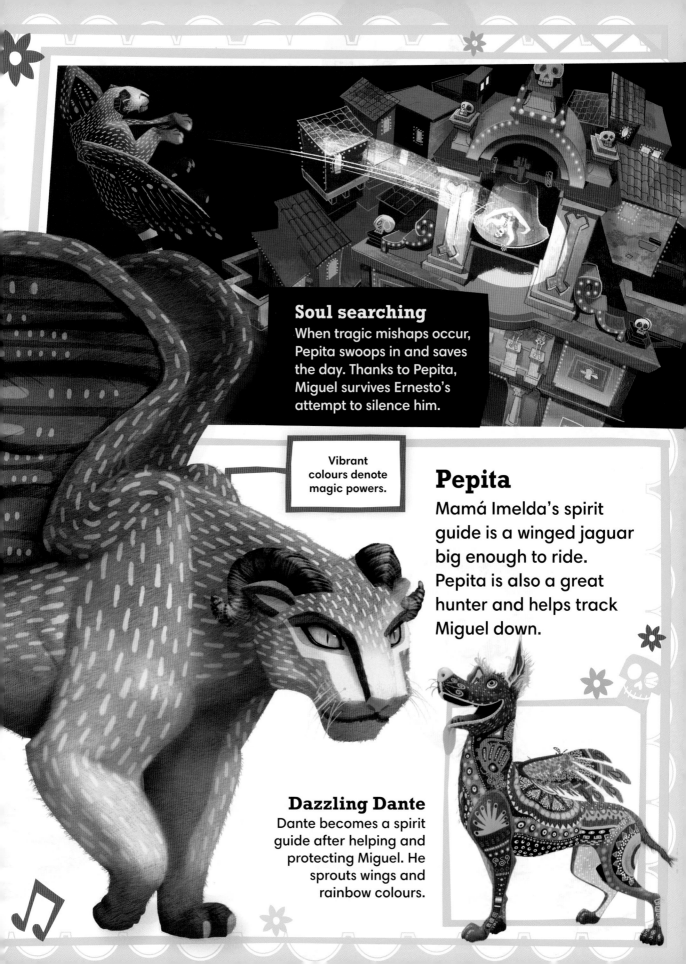

Soul searching

When tragic mishaps occur, Pepita swoops in and saves the day. Thanks to Pepita, Miguel survives Ernesto's attempt to silence him.

Vibrant colours denote magic powers.

Pepita

Mamá Imelda's spirit guide is a winged jaguar big enough to ride. Pepita is also a great hunter and helps track Miguel down.

Dazzling Dante

Dante becomes a spirit guide after helping and protecting Miguel. He sprouts wings and rainbow colours.

Pit Peril

Ernesto shows his true colours when he leaves Miguel and Hector to rot in a deep cenote, or sinkhole. The unlucky pair trade gritos – loud, passionate cries – to express the feelings in their souls. But their feelings change when rescuers appear!

Cruel de la Cruz

Ernesto orders Miguel to be thrown into the pit when the boy realises Hector's words are true. Ernesto is a liar, a killer and a song-thief! At least Miguel has Hector for company down there.

Lights glow in buildings down below

Guided to safety

The lucky prisoners are saved from the clutches of Ernesto de la Cruz when Mamá Imelda's spirit guide, Pepita, flies them to safety.

Pepita carries passengers gracefully.

Sunrise Spectacular

De la Cruz's shows are always exciting for the audience, but this year's will go down in history! Fans pelt the star with food after watching him try to silence Miguel. At last, everyone can see that de la Cruz will do anything to succeed.

De la Cruz tries to shield himself.

Rotten tomatoes thrown by angry crowd

Video nasty

The crowds are given a show they didn't expect when the TV camera is turned onto the action backstage. Thanks to Pepita, they also see Miguel's soft landing.

True or false?
De la Cruz's fans will forgive him for anything.

FALSE: They reject him after finding out his true character.

Miguel's rescue shown on huge screen

Stealing the show

When Mamá Imelda manages to snatch Hector's photo from de la Cruz, she accidentally ends up on stage with him. She shows the crowd – and de la Cruz – that she still has a few moves!

Downfall

De la Cruz brings about his own downfall when he shoves Miguel to almost certain doom. The cold-blooded de la Cruz has no idea his act is witnessed by thousands.

55

Remember Me

Memories keep the dead alive. If Hector is forgotten by the only living person who remembers him – Coco – then he will disappear in his "final death". But through his love of music, Miguel makes sure that his true ancestor will remain in the family's thoughts.

Have you heard?

Hector's friend Chicharrón turns to dust when the last living person forgets him.

Painful memory

Hector remembers his last goodbye to Ernesto as living men. Hector quit their double act, and was poisoned by de la Cruz so de la Cruz could take credit for his songs.

Our song

Hector wrote the song "Remember Me", for the young Coco, and sang it for her every night, even when they were miles apart.

Double trouble

When a spirit is almost forgotten, it becomes too weak to stand. And a living person in the realm of the dead slowly turns into a skeleton!

Happy returns

As Miguel brings her special song back to life, Mamá Coco is so happy that the memories of her devoted papá have returned.

In the picture

When Hector's face is restored to the family photo, his place in Rivera history is ensured. Now he has many Día de los Muertos celebrations to look forward to.

Forget it!

Sometimes too many memories can cause trouble. The Department of Family Reunions handles disputes between people who visit the ofrendas of too many ex-husbands and wives!

57

New baby Socorro

Miguel proudly plays guitar for his family.

Hector celebrates with his family.

Riveras have a natural flair for music.

Rivera family band

Music is back in the lives of the family in a big way. Miguel plays lead guitar, naturally, with Rosa on violin and Abel on accordion.

Musical Fiesta

A year after Miguel's dramatic trip to the Land of the Dead, the family – living and otherwise – is reunited for the next Día de los Muertos. Now things have changed, as Hector, back in the family circle, stands arm in bony arm with the rest of the Riveras.

Are you a superstar, or happy being humble?

Take this quiz to find out!

1

You need a costume for a party. Do you …

A Make your own.

B Take a costume from a family member without asking.

C Make an excuse not to go. There might be music at the party, which is never a good thing!

2

There is a big talent show in town. What are you most likely to say?

A I'd love to enter it!

B I'm going to win it!

C I'd much rather stay at home.

3

You have a chance to go to a movie, but your best friend can't afford to go with you. Do you …

A Do chores until you both have the money to go together.

B Go on your own right away. You might never get another chance!

C Forget the movie. It wasn't important anyway.

4

You tell a joke that one of your friends made up, and it gets a big laugh. Do you …

A Tell a few more. Then after the laughs say who told you them first.

B Take all the credit. After all, it's all about how well you tell it.

C Stop telling jokes as you don't really like the attention.

5

Your dog gets in your room and chews up your slippers. Do you …

A Scold him, but then give him a few treats. He's obviously hungry.

B Use it as an excuse to demand a lot of new gear from your parents.

C Ban the dog from going in your room again. Dogs should stay outside!

ANSWERS

MOSTLY 'A'
Just like **Miguel**, you like to have fun, but not if it leaves others out or feeling bad. You are a good friend who never crosses the line into selfish behaviour.

MOSTLY 'B'
You are a natural star like **Ernesto de la Cruz**. You know how to grab your moment and put yourself first. But maybe you should think of others a little?

MOSTLY 'C'
You put family values and hard work before everything else, like **Mamá Imelda**. But don't be too hard on others, and do remember to have some fun!

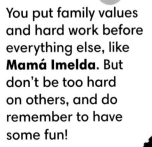

61